T0020169

AMELIA EARHART'S FINAL FLIGHT

by Megan Cooley Peterson

CAPSTONE PRESS
a capstone imprint

Published by Capstone Press, an imprint of Capstone
1710 Roe Crest Drive, North Mankato, Minnesota 56003
capstonepub.com

Library of Congress Cataloging-in-Publication Data
Names: Peterson, Megan Cooley, author.
Title: Amelia Earhart's final flight / by Megan Cooley Peterson.
Description: North Mankato, Minnesota : Capstone Press, 2022. | Series: History's mysteries | Includes bibliographical references and index. | Audience: Ages 8-11 | Audience: Grades 4-6 | Summary: "On June 1, 1937, famous pilot Amelia Earhart and her navigator, Fred Noonan, took off in their small plane. Earhart's goal was to make a record-breaking flight around the world. On the last part of the flight, they approached Howland Island to refuel. Before they could land, radio communication from Earhart stopped, and the plane disappeared. Search efforts turned up few clues. What happened to Earhart and Noonan? Explore the theories and learn why their disappearance has become one of history's greatest mysteries"-- Provided by publisher.
Identifiers: LCCN 2021023321 (print) | LCCN 2021023322 (ebook) | ISBN 9781663958730 (hardcover) | ISBN 9781666320503 (paperback) | ISBN 9781666320510 (pdf) | ISBN 9781666320534 (kindle edition)
Subjects: LCSH: Earhart, Amelia, 1897-1937--Juvenile literature. | Women air pilots--United States--Biography--Juvenile literature. | Air pilots--United States--Biography--Juvenile literature.
Classification: LCC TL540.E3 P47 2022 (print) | LCC TL540.E3 (ebook) | DDC 629.13092 [B]--dc23
LC record available at https://lccn.loc.gov/2021023321
LC ebook record available at https://lccn.loc.gov/2021023322

Editorial Credits
Editor: Carrie Sheely; Designer: Kim Pfeffer; Media Researcher: Morgan Walters; Production Specialist: Laura Manthe

Image Credits
Alamy: Historic Collection, 18; Associated Press, 5, 7, 9, 11, Charles Tasnadi, 20, Martha Irvine, 21; Getty Images: Bettmann, 12, 19, Fotosearch, 15, New York Daily News Archive, 13; National Archives and Records Administration, 27; Newscom: akg-images, 14, Album, 28, Everett Collection, Cover; Shutterstock: 3dsam79, 23, Gigi Peis, 17, Romaine W, 25

Printed and bound in the United States of America. PO4608

Table of Contents

Words in **bold** are in the glossary.

INTRODUCTION

Waiting for Amelia

On the morning of July 2, 1937, a U.S. ship waited next to Howland Island in the Pacific Ocean. The crew of *Itasca* had an important job—help pilot Amelia Earhart land her plane on the tiny island's runway. She would refuel on the island before the final part of her around-the-world flight.

The ship and island were a flurry of activity. On the *Itasca*, men sent radio signals and voice messages to help guide Earhart to the island. A canvas tent set up near the runway also housed radio equipment. Workers chased large birds from the runway. All night and into the early morning, radio operators heard bits of her radio messages. They were unsure if she heard their responses. The equipment didn't seem to be working properly.

Earhart was due to arrive a few minutes after sunrise. The crew on *Itasca* began to worry. Sunrise came and went, and there was still no sign of Earhart's plane. Where was it?

Amelia Earhart and Fred Noonan disappeared during an around-the-world flight in July 1937.

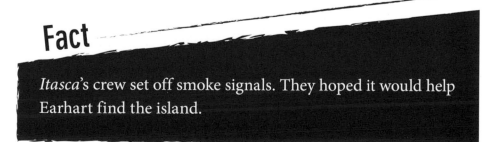

Fact

Itasca's crew set off smoke signals. They hoped it would help Earhart find the island.

CHAPTER 1

The Final Flight

Before her 1937 flight, Amelia Earhart was one of the world's most famous people. Born in Kansas in 1897, the daring pilot pushed the limits. In 1932, she had become the first woman to fly solo across the Atlantic Ocean. She soon turned her attention to a new challenge. She wanted to fly around the world.

Other pilots had flown around the world before. They had taken shorter routes in the northern part of the world. Earhart decided to stick near the **equator**. Her flight would cover 27,000 miles (43,452 kilometers). It would be the longest flight ever attempted.

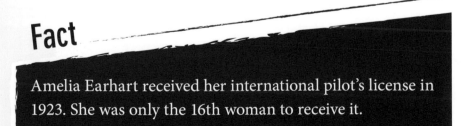

Fact

Amelia Earhart received her international pilot's license in 1923. She was only the 16th woman to receive it.

An Unlucky Start

Earhart's first around-the-world flight attempt began on March 17, 1937. Earhart and **navigator** Fred Noonan took off from Oakland, California, and headed west. Also on board were crew members Albert Mantz and Harry Manning. Earhart landed her Lockheed Electra in Honolulu, Hawaii. After refueling and some repairs, she was ready to take off for Howland Island three days later. But she crashed the plane during takeoff.

Earhart's plane took off from Oakland, California, on March 17, 1937.

Landing on Lae

After three months of repairs, the Electra was ready to fly again. On May 21, Earhart took off from Oakland and headed east. This time, only Noonan was with her. They made stops in South America, Africa, India, and southeast Asia. On June 29, they landed in Lae, New Guinea. By this point, the pair had already flown 22,000 miles (35,400 km). The end of their great adventure was in sight.

In Lae, Earhart and her team prepared for the flight to Howland Island. She told the crew on *Itasca* that she would use two radio **frequencies**. During the day, she would transmit on 6210 **kilocycles**. At night, she would switch to 3105 kilocycles.

Earhart and Noonan posed with a map of their around-the-world route.

Trouble

Before leaving Lae, Earhart and Noonan lightened the plane as much as possible. They had a full fuel load, which made the plane heavy. The heavier a plane is, the more fuel it uses. They left behind flares, smoke bombs, spare parts, and other items.

At 10:00 a.m. local time on July 2, Earhart took off. The flight to Howland Island would take about 18 hours. The island was almost 2,600 miles (4,200 km) away. Howland is a very small island. Earhart and Noonan would not be able to find it without help from the crew on *Itasca*.

Earhart's first radio messages to the ship were spotty. The sky was a bit overcast, which may have affected the signals. As sunrise neared, her messages became stronger and clearer. She seemed to be getting closer. But when the *Itasca* crew tried to radio Earhart, she didn't respond. It seemed she couldn't hear their messages. The crew tried to message Earhart using **Morse code**. Unfortunately, the *Itasca* radiomen didn't know that Earhart and Noonan could barely understand Morse code.

Earhart and Noonan (right) posed with a man just before they took off from Lae to Howland Island.

Last Words

Earhart's messages received by *Itasca*'s crew became more urgent as time passed. She reported that she was near the island and running low on fuel. She also said she had been unable to reach *Itasca* by radio. At 8:43 a.m., *Itasca* received its final radio message from Earhart. She reported that the plane was flying north and south along the line 157-337. This line of position passed over Howland Island. Amelia Earhart and Fred Noonan were never seen again. They seemed to vanish without a trace.

Itasca's crew and others on Howland Island awaited Earhart's arrival.

The Search

Within hours of Earhart's disappearance, the U.S. Navy launched a massive search. *Itasca* sailed the waters around Howland. Planes flew overhead, looking for the silver Lockheed Electra or any pieces of it. But no signs of the plane or its passengers were found. The search ended after two weeks. By early 1939, both Amelia Earhart and Fred Noonan had been declared legally dead.

The *Daily News* of New York City reported the disappearance of Earhart's plane on July 3, 1937.

CHAPTER 2

A Water Crash

Amelia Earhart disappeared more than 80 years ago. The mystery of what happened has only grown more popular over time. Why didn't she make it to Howland Island on July 2, 1937? Earhart reported she was running out of fuel. The crew on board *Itasca* guessed she ran out of fuel and crashed into the water about 100 miles (161 km) from Howland. But they didn't know if she was flying toward or away from the island.

The fate of Earhart has remained a great mystery for decades.

Amelia Earhart flew a Lockheed Electra 10E during her 1937 flight. The twin-engine plane had a wingspan of 55 feet (17 meters). Earhart replaced the extra passenger seats with extra fuel tanks.

Earhart stands in front of her Electra.

Thousands of miles of open ocean surround Howland. Earhart may have crashed into the sea. Some researchers say the Electra's design would have caused it to sink quickly. The underside of the plane had dump valves. These valves allowed a pilot to quickly dump fuel in an emergency. During the crash, water may have forced these valves open. As they quickly filled with water, the plane would have sunk. Earhart and Noonan would have drowned. The U.S. Navy agreed with this **theory**, listing Earhart's official cause of death as drowning.

If the Electra did sink, it may still sit at the bottom of the Pacific. No one has been able to find it yet. Some researchers believe the plane has likely broken down from the salt water. But they say the plane's large, heavy engines would still be **intact**.

When planes sink, some main parts can stay intact.

Fact

Earhart's plane had no shoulder harnesses. No matter where she landed, the landing would have been very rough.

CHAPTER 3

Nikumaroro

Not everyone believes Amelia Earhart drowned after a water crash. The International Group for Historic Aircraft Recovery (TIGHAR) has its own theory. They believe she crash-landed on the **coral reef** of an island called Nikumaroro. The island is about 400 miles (640 km) south of Howland. The line of position 157-337 runs through Nikumaroro. That's the same line Earhart and Noonan were flying along when they disappeared.

Nikumaroro Island is about 4.5 miles (7.2 km) long and 1.5 miles (2.4 km) wide.

TIGHAR researchers believe Earhart sent **distress signals** on frequency 3105 after the crash. These signals all seemed to come from Nikumaroro. *Itasca* and other nearby ships received signals, but they were spotty and hard to hear. U.S. Navy planes flew over Nikumaroro a week after Earhart's disappearance. They saw no signs of the plane or of Earhart and Noonan.

Fact

Several people around the United States reported hearing Earhart's voice on the radio. No one can say for sure if it was really Earhart.

Earhart's nephew and niece listen to a report on the radio about the search.

Evidence on the Island

TIGHAR researchers first investigated Nikumaroro in 1989. They did not find the Electra on the island. They believe it was swept off the reef and into the sea during high **tide**.

They have found other items on the island. In 1991, they found a small square of aluminum near where they believe she landed. During her world flight, Earhart cracked one of the plane's rear windows. The window was replaced with a piece of aluminum. Researchers measured the aluminum piece found on Nikumaroro. It fit almost perfectly over the window of a restored Lockheed Electra.

The aluminum piece and other items TIGHAR researchers found on Nikumaroro

The team also found an old campsite on the island. They discovered a metal zipper pull made in the United States between 1933 and 1936. They also found a glass jar from the 1930s. The jar may have contained cream used to fade freckles. Earhart was known for her freckles. She may have used the lotion. These personal items seem to show that a woman had camped there. But was it Amelia Earhart?

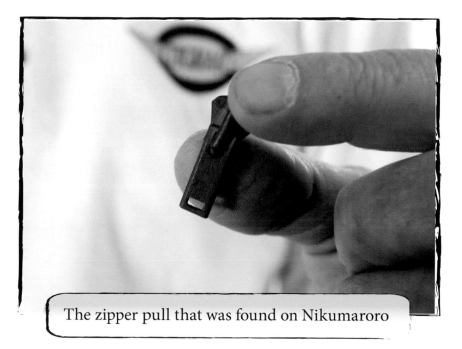

The zipper pull that was found on Nikumaroro

Human Bones

In 1940, British officials found a partial human skeleton lying under a tree on Nikumaroro. The skeleton included a skull and several other bones. Two doctors examined the bones and took measurements. They concluded the bones belonged to a male. The bones were packed away. No one has been able to find them.

Researchers took another look at the bones' measurements in 2018. They also studied Earhart's measurements by looking at photographs and clothing she wore. These researchers disagreed with the doctors' original findings. They believed the bones belonged to a woman about Earhart's size.

SEARCHING NIKUMARORO'S WATERS

Explorer Robert Ballard searched the waters for Earhart's plane around Nikumaroro in 2019. Ballard had found wreckage of the HMS *Titanic* in 1985. His team searched the ocean floor with high-tech equipment. They used a remotely operated vehicle (ROV) and **sonar**. But they didn't find any pieces of Earhart's plane.

ROVs can travel into deep ocean water to discover sunken ships and aircraft.

CHAPTER 4

The Marshall Islands

In early July 1937, two men were fishing on the Mili Atoll in the Marshall Islands. These islands lie about 800 miles (1,290 km) northwest of Howland. The men claimed a silver plane crashed on a nearby coral reef. The crash tore off the landing gear and one of the wings.

A man and woman climbed out of the plane. The man was hurt, and the woman had short hair. The men said they tried to help but couldn't understand their language. Had they come face-to-face with the famous pilot and her navigator?

The Marshall Islands include more than 1,200 islands.

Fact

In 1987, the Marshall Islands released postage stamps to remember Earhart's crash. One of them was based on reports from the eyewitnesses on Mili Atoll.

Fact or Fiction?

Some witnesses said the Japanese took Earhart and Noonan to a hospital. At the time of Earhart's crash, the Japanese controlled the Marshall Islands. They may have believed Earhart and Noonan were U.S. spies. Japanese officials reportedly took the pair to an island called Saipan. They were held there until their deaths. Some also believe the Electra was taken to Saipan and destroyed.

In 2012, a researcher uncovered a photograph taken in the 1930s on the Marshall Islands. The photo shows a woman with short hair on a dock. Her back is to the camera. Some say the woman is Amelia Earhart. Many skeptics dismissed the photo. In 2017, someone found the photo in a book published two years before Earhart disappeared. It couldn't have been Earhart in the photo.

Some people have suggested that this photo may show Earhart and Noonan on the Marshall Islands. They say the woman on the dock with her back turned may be Earhart.

THE IRENE BOLAM THEORY

According to one theory, the Japanese released Earhart. She returned to the United States and lived her life as Irene Bolam. The real Irene Bolam was also a pilot. But she looked nothing like Earhart. Bolam also denied the claim. A book claiming she was Earhart was largely discredited.

During her life, Amelia Earhart flew high as the world's most celebrated female pilot. After her death, her legend only grew. For more than 80 years, people have tried to solve the mystery. What happened to Earhart and Noonan on their last fateful flight? Until Earhart's Electra is recovered, no one can know for certain.

Earhart was famous for her flying accomplishments, and she was a role model for many women interested in becoming pilots.

The Main Theories

1. A Water Crash and Sinking

Amelia Earhart and Fred Noonan were unable to establish radio communication with *Itasca*. They ran out of fuel trying to find Howland Island. They crashed into the Pacific Ocean and drowned. Many people agree with this theory. It is also the official finding of the U.S. Navy. With so much open ocean, it's unlikely Earhart found land.

2. Castaway on Nikumaroro

Earhart and Noonan flew south of Howland and landed on Nikumaroro. They radioed for help. Earhart eventually made camp on the island. She died there. Noonan's fate after the crash is unknown. This is also one of the most widely believed theories.

3. Captured on the Marshall Islands

Earhart and Noonan crash-landed on the Marshall Islands. Japanese officials took them into custody. They later died on an island called Saipan. So far, no one has found any proof to validate this theory.

Glossary

coral reef (KOR-uhl REEF)—a strip made up of the skeletons of corals close to the ocean surface; corals are small, colorful sea creatures

distress signal (di-STRES SIG-nuhl)—a message that someone is in danger

equator (i-KWAY-tuhr)—an imaginary line around the middle of Earth

frequency (FREE-kwuhn-see)—any of the electromagnetic waves that are used for communication signals, such as radio

intact (in-TAKT)—complete and whole

kilocycle (KI-luh-sy-kul)—a unit equal to 1,000 cycles per second for expressing a frequency

Morse code (MORSS KODE)—a method of sending messages by radio using a series of long and short clicks

navigator (NAV-uh-gay-tuhr)—someone who plans an airplane's flight path; navigators read maps for pilots

sonar (SOH-nar)—a device that uses sound waves to find underwater objects

theory (THEE-ur-ee)—an idea that explains something that is unknown

tide (TYDE)—the rising and falling of the ocean up and down the shore that usually happens twice a day

Read More

Erlic, Lily. *Amelia Earhart.* New York: Smartbook Media Inc., 2021.

Jones, Grace. *People Who Changed the World: Science and Arts.* New York: Crabtree Publishing Company, 2019.

Romero, Libby. *Amelia Earhart.* New York: DK Publishing, 2020.

Shores, Erika L. *Amelia Earhart.* North Mankato, MN: Capstone, 2021.

Internet Sites

Children's Museum Indianapolis: 10 Facts About Amelia Earhart
childrensmuseum.org/blog/10-facts-about-amelia-earhart

TIGHAR
tighar.org

Time for Kids: This Is Amelia: Read the Story of Amelia Earhart
timeforkids.com/g56/this-is-amelia-earhart/

Index

Author Biography

Megan Cooley Peterson is a writer, editor, and bookworm. When she isn't writing or reading, you can find her watching movies or planning her next Halloween party. She lives in Minnesota with her husband and daughter.